The great Return

Rediscovering Workplace Culture
in a hybrid World.

Nina K Blair

Gregor Schrott

Copyright © 2024 Gregor Schrott

All rights reserved.

ISBN: 9798343826319

Disclaimer

Each organization and individual reader is responsible for making their own informed choices regarding workplace practices and policies. This book is meant to provoke thought, not to prescribe action. This book is not intended to serve as specific advice or instruction for individuals or organizations on workplace policies or practices. Readers are encouraged to consult organizational leaders, human resources professionals, legal advisors, and other relevant experts before making workplace decisions. The authors expressly disclaim any liability, damages, losses, or outcomes that may arise from the use of or reliance upon the information contained within this book, including but not limited to decisions regarding office attendance or work-from-home policies.

DEDICATION

This book is dedicated to all the people who wrote code allowing for remote work in the past 5 years. These individuals empowered us to collaborate, see and hear each other, and share the same digital canvas. To the ones ensuring stable network connections, putting in long hours upgrading hardware components in the tunnels under our cities. Composers of jingles and ringtones that we will never forget. And to the inventors of selfie light rings that made our skin glow so beautiful in dark moments. Hence, to the unsung heroes of 2020 and 2021.

CONTENTS

	Introduction	2
1	A Warning	4
2	Structure of this Book	5
3	How it all began	6
4	Three Schools	10
5	Three Places (times two)	13
6	Uniforms	16
7	Role Models	19
8	Safe Spaces	21
9	The Places in Between	25
10	EDC	27
11	Flowing with the Seasons	29
12	Beyond your Team	31
13	Enjoy the Silence	33
14	Empty Spaces	36
15	Transitioning between Worlds	39
16	Leading Others	41

THE GREAT RETURN

17	Stealing from a Popup World	44
18	Shifting the Perspective	47
19	Taking it Slow	49
20	Being Grateful	51
21	No One gets left behind	53
22	Leaders on a hybrid Ship	55
23	Accidents at the Office	56
24	The Illusion of Global Work	58
25	Micro Sabbaticals	60
26	The most wonderful Party	62
27	Riding to School together	63
28	Mirrors on the Wall	65
29	Makeup	67
30	It's not about You	69
31	Business Travel 2.0	71
32	A neutral Place	73
33	A Day in the City	75
34	A Little Bit of Nothing	77
35	Presents	79

THE GREAT RETURN

36	Big Bang Theory	81
37	Happily Ever After	83
38	So much wiser	85
39	The biggest Experiment	88
40	Perks	90
41	Superheroes	92
42	Those kind of Days	94
43	Collective Pledges	96
44	Workshop 365	98
45	A final Word	101
	The first 30 Days Diary	102
	About the Authors	112

THE GREAT RETURN

INTRODUCTION

It's been five years since Covid hit, and we were thrown into a virtual meeting world. Within the shortest time, we collaborated, connected through screens, and worked remotely in a way that seemed unthinkable before. We experimented and made mistakes. We laughed and cried together. We re-learned work and created a 'new normal' that we got used to. Private schedules merged with work, and the old dichotomy of 'work' and 'life' blurred like an incredible impressionist artwork in a virtual museum. Colourful. Individualistic. No remote workers' world seemed like the one of the people living next door—the end of uniformity.

Then we realized that more than being online is needed; we miss out on something. We longed for an old friend: meeting others in the corporate hallways—the 'normal' before the 'new normal.' So we felt the ground of long-forgotten commutes under our feet again and the weight of backpacks on our shoulders. We were exploring empty office spaces, step by step, entering territory that felt so unnatural, so distant, so alien.

We start wondering what to make of this while standing in line for lunch with hundreds of colleagues. We wonder if and how to recreate a 'new old normal.' What do we want to leave behind at home, and what do we want to bring here? What to preserve and what to forget? We wonder how we have changed and work has changed since we left.

THE GREAT RETURN

May these pages help you find answers, get a good start, feel unprecedented levels of emotional safety outside your home, and create an environment that gets the best out of you.

Read it alone or as a team. Keep it neat and clean, or splatter the pages with annotations and drawings. Rip out all you don't like and take what is precious.

Nina and Gregor.
At the home office, December 2024

1 A WARNING

Books, including this one, often paint the world in black and white and fuel stereotypical thinking. They take shortcuts and oversimplify. In the following 100 pages, you will find all of the above. This is because the topic is very complex and highly individualistic. No person feels or thinks the same way as another; even one person's views about where and how to work are subject to constant change. We make experiences, reflect, adapt, and start all over again. The objective of this book is to support the in-between moments of reflection. To offer some perspectives that have not been on your mind before. To stimulate and hopefully to surprise.

The prime prospects for this book are members of the ‚big corporate' tribe. They might find it easy to relate to what we adress. People working as freelancers who have experienced and thrived in hybrid settings for decades might not always understand why this is worth discussing. We would encourage them, together with those who embraced startup environments, to see these reflections as an opportunity better to understand their corporate colleagues' hearts and minds. Their feeling of being lost. Their search for a new balance between different modes of working. To find an answer on how to cope with all the changes that have been thrown at them. It might make them more sensible when dealing with them, and most of all, you might be able to support them with all you have learnt about hybrid work years ago.

2 STRUCTURE OF THIS BOOK

If you ask your favorite AI about ideal structures for a book like this, it will provide you with various ways to guide the reader to a solid outcome. We, however, decided not to force the thoughts in this book into a rigid system. Our guide aims to help you determine how to orchestrate different locations and modes of working for you and those around you. And there are several ways to achieve this.

You can concisely transmit well-thought-through arguments, including a checklist at the end to provide you, our beloved readers, with clear guidance on how to make this a success. Or you could put on your coaching hat and start asking questions. To get your heads ringing. To induce and support a process of deep reflection and thought. To start thinking, experiment, then listen to your heart, adjust, and do it all over again. To have a tool to turn to after all the positive episodes and adverse incidents you went through, along the way back to the office and the places in between.

We believe the best way to achieve this is to throw different chapters at you. To ask the same questions again, circle, and return to the places we have already been. To surprise you. To disturb you. And we do this by using language that comes straight from our mouth. Like a podcast. Like a blog. To do everything in our power to design an experience for you that will help you find your answers. The only structure we provide is within each chapter. At the end of each one, you will find some questions for reflection, followed by some space for your thoughts and notes.

Hence, trust the process and the authors that this will lead you to a good place. To make this a comfortable journey, we will start by looking at how it all began.

3 HOW IT ALL BEGAN

Let's time-travel back six years ago. Until 2020, we have lived in a world where the corporate badge around your neck witnessed a routine of entering and leaving 'the office'—swiping in the morning when entering a building and in the evening when commuting back 'home.' Probably another two swipes when grabbing lunch 'outside.' This was the heartbeat of the year's days, weeks, and months. Some business travel to other offices in between, and a couple of retreats broke up the pattern.

If things went wild, we stretched working hours and utilized commute time to call people or to dial into telephone conferences (with an actual phone) from 'home.' Another break from the routine took place in case of private emergencies, when cars stayed longer in the repair workshop than expected, or once we injured an ankle during a nightly run and could not make it to the corporate halls. We felt terrible for not being able to 'show up,' it seemed that everyone (including us) believed we did not contribute 100% once we were not present at 'the office.'

And then came Covid. Overnight, we found ourselves confined to our private homes. After a short phase of shock and loss of orientation, we started to mimic and recreate office environments. How do you set up shop for days in a row rather than open up a laptop on a couch or sit at the dinner table for 2 hours in the evening? We experienced the difference between a chair you sit on sometimes and 'professional office furniture' that has been through decades of ergonomics testing. Many things that we took for granted before, like an it service desk that you can quickly step by, we started to miss dearly. And we learned together. Little hacks and recommendations about digital equipment have allowed us to become more savvy in holding

THE GREAT RETURN

virtual spaces. We experimented. Not one week without something new. A feature we have not been aware of before, a new way of doing things. We were all in this together.

And then we started getting used to it. So when the world outside returned to normal, something strange happened. We realized that staying home had many benefits we didn't want to let go of. We did not need to spend time on commutes anymore. We could handle errands far more efficiently than before, like opening the door for parcel delivery and avoiding several stickers and failed delivery attempts. We made a quick run to the grocery store during regular office hours. We could eat the things we liked containing the ingredients we liked out of kitchens we liked at prices that were far lower than in corporate food halls or at restaurants. A short workout or run at lunchtime? No problem. Were we switching clothes three times a day? A dream is coming true.

And we became far more efficient in virtual gatherings. Less energy is needed to hold our focus for more extended periods and easily switch between meetings fluidly. And we started to personalize our desks again after years of 'clean desk policies.' Things became cozy again. We were holding our favorite mugs in our hands without having to hide them in the corner of the corporate kitchen drawers. It seemed that our keyboards, mice, and laptops went through a decontamination phase, qualifying them to stay in our homes like shoes that are only worn inside and never see the dirty streets outside. Our perfect private office world at home…

… until the one virtual meeting that did not go too well. The one conversation that, no matter how hard we tried, fell short of being truly connected. Feeling the frustration of not being

THE GREAT RETURN

understood. Not on a rational level but from the heart. An excuse that did not come across. Condolences that we felt somehow did not reach our conversation partner. Or the moment we realized something was missing that had always been given in face-to-face conversations.

After this first incident, the perfect 'home office' world never felt the same again. We found ourselves in another situation that suddenly had a wrong tune to it, and another until we realized that an exclusive remote work setup might not be a good idea despite all its benefits. We longed for inter-personal connections again. We missed looking each other in the eye, not through the lenses of our digital cameras, but in real life. To use our human ability to assess over 16,000 unique facial expressions in the blink of an eye. To feel each other with all our emotions.

So we packed our bags and went to experience 'day 1' at the corporate office again. Returning to a world where we would exchange our private desks for the ones we left behind in a hurry.

First, some individuals, then small groups; meanwhile, more and more people are showing up at their old business theatres. Some on single days, spontaneous. Others are embracing a more regular rhythm of dedicated days on-premise and off. And here we are today.

Our first steps feel clumsy, as do the ones from our employers. We have not yet 'cracked' it. We have not yet achieved the level of togetherness that we expected. And it seems that both 'sides' are doing their best to figure out how to create a perfect hybrid cocktail—a new drumbeat for the years to come.

THE GREAT RETURN

Some employers transformed their office environment into an Instagrammable haven while we were out. Fully delivering a life-stylish experience, the new Envy offices aim to make you feel at home. Classic chairs made way for couches, eradicating the sterility of decades. The old color palette was updated to include a more contemporary selection of brand-strengthening Pantone choices. All hope to lure workers back to the office and create a feeling of togetherness.

For others, returning to the old office address feels like reconnecting to an old world: same buildings, same offices, same furniture. But one thing has changed: we are not the same. We are left with more options and the burden of solving the riddle that made you put the book in your hands: how to rediscover workplace culture in a hybrid world?

4 THREE SCHOOLS

Right now, there seem to be three groups with distinct mindsets: the office lovers, the office haters, and the undecided.

The office lovers. Members of this tribe have been counting the days until they were allowed back into the corporate halls. Mainly on the extroverted side, they felt absolute joy to camp in the kitchen areas again. To bump into people. To listen to others. To have meetings in person with real people. They will not stop telling everyone how great it is to be back in the office and support any activities to bring people back. And, of course, they already complain about being too busy having to talk to so many people that they really miss the solitude of their home office (which is absolutely not true), but a grand narrative. Members of this tribe also tend to forget to dial into virtual meetings and online participants because they focus on all the people in the room with excitement. If you were to name a stereotyped persona, 'Office Olivia' might be a fitting name for this group.

On the other side of the spectrum are the office haters. They feel no incentive to return to the 'old offices.' From the bottom of their heart, they believe that the company gets the most out of their every hour by working in isolation or being virtually connected to their colleagues worldwide. They see the company through the eyes of their VPN. Anecdotal evidence suggests that the majority might be found in deep tech and identify as inside-oriented, on the thinking side. They do not participate in the current debate (at least not in an open, visible forum). Did their world change significantly during COVID-19?

THE GREAT RETURN

A dream finally came true: not having to 'show up in person' all the time, being forced to listen to endless monologues in big group meetings, and not being allowed to do some 'meaningful work' at the side. 'Virtual Victor' might be a nice name for a persona.

And then there is you, the readers of this book. The undecided. The ones who have yet to make up their mind. The ones aiming to get clarity about the potentials and limitations of each way of working and orchestration. Sensing that trustful relationships almost always start with people working together in a physical space but that there is so much more to consider when making a choice on relearning hybrid. Right now, they listen to many voices, explore, and make up their mind. What a beautiful place to be in.

THE GREAT RETURN

Questions for thought:

1. If you think about the people around you. Which group do they belong to?

2. Have you noticed a change in their behavior in the past months?

3. What would be the best way to bring all extremists to work together?

5 THREE PLACES (TIMES TWO)

Over 30 years ago, in the early days of groupware, Ellis, Gibs, and Rein created a beautiful time/space taxonomy of communication. Building on this, we can differentiate between three locations (at home, at the office, or another place) and if the actors are physically present or communicate virtually. This leaves us with six stereotype situations:

1. Working physically from the office (e.g., a meeting with all participants in one room).

2. Working virtually from the home office (e.g., dialing into a virtual conference with colleagues).

3. Working virtually from the office (e.g., participating in a virtual conference).

4. Working virtually while commuting (e.g., dialing into a virtual conference).

5. Working physically while commuting or at a place that is neither the corporate nor the home office (e.g., meeting a colleague in a cafe or a long walk in the forest).

6. Working physically from the home office (e.g., meeting colleagues at home).

We could further refine this by having some participants be at the same place and others participating virtually. In in light of most corporate cultures and habits, inviting colleagues to your home might be the exception rather than the default setting (case number six above).

THE GREAT RETURN

To make things even more fun, none of the modes above seem exclusive throughout the day (morning at the office, afternoon at home). However, in most cases, we decide on a duration of one day. Over the past months, we also got the impression that people know at least for the coming week where they plan on spending the day and then refine all the fantastic contradicting factors we will encounter in the remainder of the book. Will these choices always be communicated? Anecdotal evidence suggests that many 'oh, you are at home today / at the office' can still be heard in virtual conversations. It seems that to be aligned with our colleagues is a game of probabilities.

Our world to decide is not black and white, and the chances that we communicate are also non-digital. What a great setup to design things flexibly or to create massive chaos and confusion. One person's dream is another person's nightmare.

THE GREAT RETURN

Questions for thought:

1. How did you split across all stereotype situations look like in the past three months?

2. Has there been a pattern to it?

3. If so, how did you communicate about it?

4. What makes each of the six settings valuable for you?

5. What kind of work qualifies for which of the six settings?

6. What is the current default preferred mode of working for your colleagues and why?

THE GREAT RETURN

6 UNIFORMS

The old dichotomy of 'dressing for the office' and 'dressing at home' no longer holds. Not only interviews with Raf Simons but a subtle shift in Scott Schumann's Instagram Stream stand witness to the plurality of clothes we wrap around our bodies these days.

With 'casual Friday' hitting the mainstream in the late 1990s, the door opened for 'business casual' combinations of items beyond the clear judgment of being appropriate for corporate hallways. With more freedom to choose, mix, and match, a new universe opened beyond the established implicit uniforms. There have been some corporate guardrails. However, we had an unprecedented opportunity to self-express according to our personality, taste, or mask that we wanted to wear.

And then came 2000. The moment tech billionaires surfaced and public media dedicated significant attention to the dress code of CEOs on stage. Things went even more casual (low-key rich nerds). Turtlenecks and T-shirts made the headlines. The color palette consisted of black, white, grey, and navy. No visible logos. Other industries and regions started to adopt, slowly but surely.

Fast forward to 2020. First went the shoes, then the hairstyle (lack of access to your trusted artist), and it seemed that on some days, we chose to stay completely 'off camera' because we did not feel like being stared at, being recorded, being judged. A benefit that never existed in the world before when sitting in meeting rooms surrounded by colleagues.

THE GREAT RETURN

And then we started selling our beloved more formal 'office wear' including exclusive laptop bags. All the major reselling sites are bursting with wardrobes that would have been aspirational in the old days. So, with our bodies walking around the corporate halls sometimes again, what should we expect? Here are some predictions:

1. There will be more attention on how we dress because fewer bookshelves are in the back to distract, and we can see the whole body rather than the top 50 cm through a screen.

2. Everyone seems to have gone down the spiral of 'casual home dress' and feels trapped between falling back to old styling habits or resurfacing in a new way. You are not alone.

3. Tech is not going away. With the AI gods unleashed, tech style has manifested as the 'new uniform.' Unisex, of course. However, you might dress your avatar as you please.

4. It's about you. Assuming everyone has lost control and feels about 'what is right,' why not go straight for 'dopamine dressing' (i.e., putting on whatever gives you good vibes in the morning)?

5. Judging from the exploding bookshelf on coaching and self-help during the pandemic years, the clothes you put on can be a wonderful part of your new personal brand. Your new 'you.'

THE GREAT RETURN

6. A changed catwalk. These days, we are up to six new collections per year for most fashion houses. This means over 20 collections have passed since we left the offices in 2020. It's probably worth a look at how people on the street dress these days.

7. A new crowd. Gen Z (and their social media friends) have entered the workforce. They will bring a refreshing new style to the old hallways. On top of that, this is the first time they have adjusted to an office environment. Be prepared for some inspirational surprises.

8. Returning home. Let's assume you adjusted your wardrobe to return to the office and join virtually from home. Will your new 'home-style' mimic the new 'office style' inspired by the old 'home style' in the first place?

Questions for thought:

1. Can you relate to the eight previous statements?

2. What do they mean for you?

7 ROLE MODELS

Life is easier if we stand on the shoulders of others. Several groups had already managed to shape-shift back from home to an office environment long before we were forced to leave the office, and this might be an invaluable source of good practices for us.

One prominent group is parents going on maternity leave. Depending on labor laws, culture, and personal preference, colleagues leave the office for some time.

Colleagues were taking a sabbatical, checking out of the career marathon, and enjoying some time getting a different perspective. For example, it is common practice in academia to have a research sabbatical every 7 years, like clockwork.

Aside from voluntary leaves, sometimes fate takes its toll. We face illness (or someone we love and care for). Several corporations have standard practices to facilitate a successful return to the workforce.

People are leaving their working teams due to a 'special assignment.' They disappear, only leaving behind their name on a locker in the office to return in flesh and blood after a couple of months.

Hence, before 'the great Return,' there were 'small Returns,' and there is hardly a chance that you had not witnessed this.

THE GREAT RETURN

Questions for thought:

1. What have been good practices in observing people returning after more prolonged absences?

2. How would your 'first 100 days' look like after a long sabbatical? What are the first three things you would do?

THE GREAT RETURN

8 SAFE SPACES

There seem to be two stereotypes of participants in remote (online) conversations: on camera or not. Sometimes, the conversation setting determines whether you bring your selfie-self to the meeting or just your voice. In virtual rooms, over 100 people tend to behave differently than in a setting with 5-7 participants, which also seems to have a different 'netiquette' and tonality than two people talking to each other. Reciprocity is often at work (if everybody is showing their face....) and the topic of the conversation (think development dialogues on the one hand and a presentation about the latest financial numbers as a meeting without faces).

So, what happens if you activate your camera? You allow people to enter the setting you are in at that moment. You invite people to your living room if that is your 'home office' workplace. They can glimpse a world that tells a lot about you. Your furniture style, what books are on your shelves, if animals are running around, probably artwork, and sometimes people that are not part of the conversation and not part of the company you work for might enter the scene. You share.

Since deciding whether to activate your camera or not is a difficult choice, the creators of virtual collaboration tools have gifted us the feature of virtual backgrounds. Whether nice pictures of nature (often a conversation opener), selected pieces from your digital photo stream, or corporate (team) backgrounds that entered the scene around 2022 on a large scale. They all allow you to have a step-in-between camera on or off. They allow you to share your face but not the world you don't want to share.

THE GREAT RETURN

Sometimes, you don't want to make other participants uncomfortable (think shaking cameras for longer than 5 minutes), while at other places, you want to keep a wall between your 'professional self' and 'private self.'

We would argue that staying 'in the dark' and not sharing your live picture adds to your personal safety. That's why hotlines for troubled teenagers, for example, still receive mainly voice calls even though video-supported calls have been available on a large scale for years.

Now add AI-induced tools for recording and automated transcription to the mix, and it seems that we work in three different worlds:

Personal. A wonderful private, cozy world at home' that provided warmth and personal safety. We are opening a digital window to the world 'out there,' but we don't invite everyone into this world, and definitely not in person. Before remote work, this challenge did not exist. We left our personal safe spaces, locked the doors well, and then went on a journey into another world, entering world number two.

Public. We expose ourselves to the public world when commuting to enter another safe space again in bright light. Open for all eyes to see. Sometimes, the impact can be limited by wearing oversized sunglasses or using cars instead of public transport.

Corporate. Gates, security guards, fences. A safe space as well. Different from the personal one, however, it is also distinct from walking down the street or sitting in a subway on the way to work.

THE GREAT RETURN

Three shades of safety and levels of being exposed.

Things get pretty interesting if you talk to corporate security officers these days (hence, the people who see and handle things most civilians don't know exist). For them, the three worlds look different. While there is agreement on world number 2 (the public world), especially business travel, for them, world number 1 (personal) and world number 3 (corporate) are upside down when it comes to safety. Statistics show that over the past three years, the number of accidents, specifically severe accidents, has increased with people working from their homes. There is no one checking up on electricity or office furniture. There are no regular fire drills where everyone ends up in the parking lot, no first responders per department, and no medical department on-site if you don't live next door to an ER of a hospital. All of those reasons seem to be pretty obvious. One thing that surprised us was the comment on awareness of risks. It seems that in our cozy private world, we don't see danger coming. There are few cues on being alert, like the signs that warn you not to use a cell phone while taking the stairs. There is different lighting. Your senses are more alert when being on corporate land.

The same holds for information security, where we assume that all people living in our neighborhoods can hardly be suspected to be interested in listening to our conversations or caring about what we write on our laptops or discuss with others. It's a low-guard world.

THE GREAT RETURN

Questions for thought:

1. Which environment makes you truly comfortable and why?

2. What role do other people play in that?

3. What would it take to make you absolutely safe in all three worlds?

THE GREAT RETURN

9 THE PLACES IN BETWEEN

According to most social media streams, we should have written this book in a cafe. Smooth music from a 60s vinyl turntable, drip coffee, minimalistic furniture, and a silver notebook right next to the most beautiful piece of cake you have ever seen. There is probably some soft, drizzling rain out on the street that you can see through the open window. A blue waxed canvas tote stands beside the table with a worn-down field notebook peeking out, revealing months of intense research. A dream office outside my home and absolutely outside of any corporate building. A dedicated destination for 'that kind of work.'

Well, there are a couple of challenges associated with such a place. First, it may be too perfect. As you will never be able to meditate in a picturesque Japanese Garden because the breathtaking beauty will distract you painfully, an ideal cafe might not lead to excellent writing and productivity. Adding some interesting guests, and here goes all concentration (that might be one of the reasons for cafe-house-sound-libraries available at your favorite streaming service to take them home with you).

However, there is hope. Many coffee house chains provide absolute uniformity and deliver exactly what the brand of choice promises. No distracting surprises. Even the interior design will adhere to the defined color palette and provide an experience that is available around the globe. Your little in-between world. Something outside of the corporate halls but not your living room.

THE GREAT RETURN

Questions for thought:

1. What have been the places in-between of your youth?

2. What were the places in between during your university years?

3. What have been your places in between in the past three years?

4. What made all the places above special to you?

THE GREAT RETURN

10 EDC

Unlike the first-row guests at fashion shows who travel very light, we tend to carry bags around with 'stuff.' While at the home office, we have been working out of a massive and convenient self-storage space; we now must consciously choose what to bring to the office.

Many lifestyle blogs have created a dedicated category for these items we carry in our bags, with the straightforward acronym 'Every Day Carry, EDC.' While our great great grandfather Ötzi (the one getting shot while crossing the Alps 3,500 BCE) used to carry warm coal/ember at all times to be able to light a fire if need be, it seems that these days our packing choices are more guided by what we 'want to bring' rather than what we 'have to bring.' Despite several waves of attempting to become minimalists, we are still drowning in stuff (printed version of this book vs. the ebook included). Option paralysis every morning on the days we travel to the corporate office. It is probably even more challenging because we have not yet found a rhythm or a well-trained routine. And with the threat looming above us to forget the one piece of equipment that will make or break your day (think joining a virtual conference at the office without headphones while all meeting rooms are booked).

THE GREAT RETURN

Questions for thought:

1. If you can only bring five items, which ones will that be?

2. What items do you feel comfortable sharing, and which ones are 'personal'?

3. Is there anything to gain from the way you get ready? Do you use a pilot-style checklist or throw all you can grab in an oversized duffle before you rush out?

11 FLOWING WITH THE SEASONS

Depending on your region, the impact of seasons differs significantly. The more you move away from the equator towards the poles, the more likely your working schedule is impacted by the hours of sun available. The work schedule will also adapt in several countries with stark differences in temperatures and sunlight between summer and winter. Shorter days in the summer and longer hours in the winter. This might have an impact on your decision to work hybrid.

Road conditions vary, and your favorite means of transportation go with them. Are you riding your favorite bike or an old car, skipping the bus walking? Which shoes do you wear for walking, and in which season and weather? What if you decided to spend all day in the home office, but the warm autumn day simply 'pulls you outside'?

How much cozy do you need? Unfortunately, most building codes for corporate offices do not allow for open fireplaces these days. Hence, if that's your poison, why not take the meeting to an old hotel that allows for some time travel (or simply turning up the floor heating system at home might also do the job)?

THE GREAT RETURN

Questions for thought:

1. What does my inner clock tell me about making a hybrid choices along the four seasons?

2. What are the most precious outdoor spots for work-related conversations in the summertime/winter?

3. What is your perfect 'operating temperature,' and where do you find it?

12 BEYOND YOUR TEAM

The default working mode seems to be 'in teams', i.e., a group of people you spend most of your time with. Hence, it seems intuitive to delegate the decision about how the perfect hybrid work cocktail should look to the team. You and your colleagues decide what's best to maximize every hour companies pay you. Flexible and with the hypothesis that you are the best judge for this decision.

Each team is unique, with different personalities, serving one purpose at a specific time. If one of the variables changes, e.g., a new team member joining, you might adjust the default working mode, for example, deciding to work from the corporate office so that the person gets a good onboarding and feels genuinely welcome.

This, of course, requires the team to be able to come to one decision. Not in a sense that all team members have to adhere to the same working modes but rather to have a joint agreement that all team members hold each other responsible for. Chances seem high that this can work. Probably, with the support of a capable person moderating the conversation and capturing agreements, it is making them explicit for the group, ensuring consent and support in defining rituals, coping with things not working out as planned, or adjusting in light of changed circumstances.

So far, so good and fitting the current 'Leadership Zeitgeist' in assuming that people know best what's right for them; delegation is needed to decide on the best way to generate output and ensure the maximum outcome. And here comes the challenge.

THE GREAT RETURN

Teams do not operate in isolation but interlink with other entities within organizations. Hence, they might be well advised to mirror their agreements with their significant working others. It also seems to be a good idea to 'steal with pride' from the experiences others have had, the organization's collective wisdom, and external impulses like this book.

However, the biggest challenge and chance lies in external effects. The things that the team does not see or has a hard time anticipating. I bumped into an intern from another department kitchen department and learned about a new insight. It took five minutes to converse with someone from the controlling department who attended a training session with you some time ago and who you always wanted to catch up with. All the things you do not see coming, don't plan for. All the surprises are opportunities to exchange and foster bonds. And that means that despite all the best efforts, there might be treasures hidden beyond what our eyes can see. We might get stuck in a local optima.

Questions for thought:

1. What are good buckets / occasions to exchange with other teams?

2. Who is the most suitable 'coordination wizard' that can facilitate alignment with oher teams?

3. How can you capture and harvest valuable 'accidents'?

13 ENJOY THE SILENCE

Most of us are blessed with jobs that require different styles of working. We can only excel if we can master deep as well as fast thinking. Suppose we can shift between immersing deeply into problems and using our gifts of spontaneous intuition. For some, these changes occur daily, for some every couple of hours. Some are lucky to be able to plan for different phases, but in many cases, external forces are throwing different tasks at us on concise notice. Depending on your personality, this might be refreshing and fun or driving you crazy.

However, our environment's noise seems to impact our ability to go deep and concentrate significantly. Aside from the ones still remembering missing a plane for the first time because they got lost while reading at the gate, let's assume that different levels and types of noise benefit various kinds of work.

No noise. Have you ever been invited to a music studio? We are not talking about sitting at the table to record a podcast but standing in a vocal booth with a big pop shield and microphone in front of you? Something interesting happens there. Once you enter 'the box' you sense that something is off. Its a hard to describe the feeling of being lost. Sudden silence. Something is absorbing all the noise. The background sound of the air condition is gone. Noises from outside traffic: gone. The noise of your clothes rustling: gone. The world suddenly becomes less warm. Less comfy. You shut your eyes for a minute (big mistake), and there it is: you can hear your blood flow through your arteries. You swallow and realize you are hearing things you missed out on before. After a few minutes in this environment, you know that feeling utterly detached from the outside world is not the kind of silence that gets the best out of ordinary people. It's too silent.

THE GREAT RETURN

Low noise. Hence, sometimes we love to take 25-40 decibels off the daily sound waves that clash against our ears to foster concentration; however, it's about dimming, not eliminating all noise. None of the active noise cancellation devices (whether you are the over-ear, on-ear, or in-ear type) will promise absolute silence. It is about leaving some noise, and there is a strong demand for that. One out of four US Households owns an active noise-canceling device already. And the need for personal bubbles of silence seems to be a side effect of us returning to office in masses. There is hardly any week without a new company offering 'silent' booths (aka pods). Overnight, all the empty corporate spaces we used to host receptions have been filled up with rectangular boxes to escape the noise of the office and limit the passive participation rate in our virtual meetings. Something in-between using a high-quality speaker in a conference room or sitting at your desk, dialing into a call with headphones. A little island of silence and privacy. Wood, natural fabrics, soft light, glass door. Low noise instead of no noise.

But this is only half the story. We spoke about blocking disturbing noises to allow for more focus. How about using sounds and music to get us in the right mood for specific tasks and activities? The older readers of this book might remember legendary Ronny Coleman pushing thousands of pounds while saying, 'Lightweight baby, lightweight'. Metroflex gym was no place of silence. You could hear people swearing, suffering, and weights clanking. Even 30 years later, voices like David Goggins 'Who's gonna carry the boats?' suggest not stimulating yourself with music but staying away from headphones while working out. While Tara Styles or Adriene Mishler (Yoga with Adriene) allow for smooth background music, traditionalists like Kino MacGregor would suggest that you listen to your breathing and don't mimic the armies of workout music-loving enthusiasts who

THE GREAT RETURN

will never hear the sound of their feet on the treadmill right next to you—linking their music's bpm (beats per minute) to their heartbeat. An antidote for suppressing music but to use it for higher performance. To get into a good rhythm. The base for all the HIIT presents that Dr. Tabata gifted us with. The 125bpm always felt so right, allowing us to dance the night away in the clubs worldwide.

All the sounds that get you in the right mood. That opens the door to a dream world, just to disappear after a while. Little helpers for the first 15 minutes before you are fully immersed in the tasks at hand. Like dimming the light, putting on some songs from Ryuichi Sakamoto, and writing these pages without listening to the music anymore. At home.

Questions for reflection:

1. What is your favorite place to find solitude?

2. How can you consciously decide about and optimize your sound-environment?

3. What are visual cues for others to signal that you require some undisturbed time?

THE GREAT RETURN

14 EMPTY SPACES

Whether the hype around minimalism and the incredible work of Marie Kondo is going back to a healthy normal, returning to the office is an excellent opportunity to reflect on the free space around us.

On the one hand, we have a unique chance to de-clutter our homes again. With our bodies returning to the office for most days, we no longer need the big monitor on the desk or the ergonomic office chair, and we may even be able to let go of the one room that we spent so many hours in past years. We will gain space that was not available in past years.

So what to do with it? We could preserve it and create some 'meaningful emptiness'. A source of calmness and clarity. Where the mind can rest. A space where things are being left empty on purpose. Or we decide to downsize and move into a new home with a smaller footprint. The flat next door has one room less on the blueprint, leaving you with a good conscience (less emissions) and more money in your pocket (whether you have to spend it on the commute is another story). Since you probably won't entirely move back to the corporate office, we might keep a little 'pop-up office' at hand.

And then there is the office space. Most likely, you are one of many people setting foot back into the corporate office world. Let's assume that you still recognize the space and furniture of the office. Chances are high that someone has 'taken over' your favorite corner while you were out. That someone has made use of all the free space suddenly available. Hence, you face the question of whether you want to 'claim back' your space.

THE GREAT RETURN

If you proactively choose a particular space or apply a more nomad style 'I sit where there is free space' approach.

Then, some corporations have decided to reduce unused office space (see your private choice above), anticipating permanent hybrid work settings. Things might get cozy due to smaller overall office footprints. Interestingly, things have always been comfortable in several corners of this world. Even in the glorious 80s, no one would have expected lavish office square feet per person in the skyscrapers of Hong Kong, Japan, or NYC. That has been a luxury throughout Europe and parts of the United States.

But there is another movement, further reducing personal office space. In recent years, we have observed a shift, especially in big tech, to maximize 'general space' and reduce 'individual space'. In light of the inability to foresee individual choices and predict what type of work from what place of work will take place for how long and the choices all of us make, it makes sense to maximize flexibility. Having one open space that can be used for people to enjoy a poke bowl by themselves, celebrate success, have a mentoring session, or dial into a virtual conference seems like a good thing. However, this leaves less space for classic individual desk settings.

Hence, two sides of the physical space coin are attached to the great return to office and another aspect that adds to the puzzle of hybrid work design we are trying to solve.

THE GREAT RETURN

Questions for reflection:

1. What is the minimal setup that you need in next 6 months?

2. How can you turn this into a tremendous de-cluttering exercise?

3. How has the tonality of your home office world already changed in the past 6 months?

4. What would help you reset your working practices at the office in light of changed office spaces?

5. What can you learn from visitors coming to your office from another region?

15 TRANSITIONING BETWEEN WORLDS

Whether you embrace sacred leadership and call upon the spirits regularly or prefer standing with both feet on the ground, creating rituals for entering and leaving one or the other space might be of great value to you. Having defined rites of passage allows one to let go of one's working mode or prepare for what is to come, shortening the time needed to warm up.

Corporate life is full of rituals. Grabbing a joint drink at a bar after the team successfully hit a milestone in a project. Taking a short walk around the parking lot after lunch. Going through your calendar of the day while standing in line for a coffee-to-go before entering the corporate perimeter. Switching shoes. Cleaning your desk on a Tuesday morning to feel comfortable in the office for the next three days. Throwing a tab into the dishwasher and starting the machine with you being the last one leaving the office in the evening...

How can we make more use of such rituals when entering and leaving the home office, the corporate office and the spaces in between? How do we maximize the chances of becoming 100% immersed within the shortest time and getting the best out of each world?

THE GREAT RETURN

Questions for reflection:

1. What are your most precious routines?

2. What are the most precious routines for the team you work in?

3. Which physical cues indicate a transition for you?

4. What would be the best way to start a day in the home/corporate office?

16 LEADING OTHERS

Getting clarity for ourselves on the preferred hybrid mix takes work. So how about taking that decision for others? Guiding a team or larger organization?

In leaving the dark days of transactional management behind us, we acknowledge that a) the answer to every question is in the room and b) that it's hardly always the same person holding the correct answer. On top of that, we have learned that with ever-increasing uncertainty and shorter tipping points of markets, no answer will stay valid for an extended period. We have to take an iterative approach, including constant adjustment along the way.

Hence, an excellent approach might be to have dialogue and understand where everybody is coming from. Second, to make any agreement transparent, and third, to put mechanisms in place when to question the deal again and to revise and adjust.

And all of this is easier said than done. It might be fair to assume that only a faction of us understands our hybrid-mix preferences already. We need time to exchange and reflect and come up with an opinion on the optimal design for us for the time being. Then, we must agree on what's best for the group. Depending on your company culture, this might range from consensus-driven approaches to top-down mandates. Some groups will delegate the ownership and decisions to individuals, while others might choose a more central coordinating mechanism. In any case, it seems crucial to document well what has been decided or explicitly not being decided.

THE GREAT RETURN

As a third step, groups should decide on when the agreements should be questioned again and require some adjustment. Either based on the changed environment or preference of the group. For example, some team members cant't join a physical meeting at the office and plan to dial in virtually. Team members on the premise might decide to split up and dial in individually and virtually to ensure all participants feel the same comfort and changes are high for the same share of voice. If this occurs more often, the group might want to change an agreement put in place before on how to hold meetings (e.g., if more than X members don't make it, then we switch to a virtual one). Leaders might have the ultimate responsibility to provide spaces where such coordination can occur, acknowledging that they also don't hold the answer, committing to any minimal viable hybrid model that gets the best out of the group at one point.

THE GREAT RETURN

Questions for reflection:

1. What agreements does the team have in place for when and where to work? What are the 'unspoken rules of the team'?

2. Do you understand the underlying motivation of each team member's hybrid preferences? What is a suitable format for getting clarity?

3. What can you learn from other teams on documenting agreements?

4. What is an excellent rhythm to question and adjust existing agreements?

THE GREAT RETURN

17 STEALING FROM A POPUP WORLD

It seems that more and more physical events occur at locations with a 'pop-up' character, like a store that utilizes an empty lot at a prime location for a limited period. Tenants could be some big brands that want to reinforce their brand image. Manufacturers are entering a new market and wanting to test the waters in a live environment or an alternative artisan artist project that would never have the means to enter a long-term rental agreement on high street.

When entering such a microcosmos, there is an exceptional ring to it. You can sense the freshness, the commitment, the love in the details. You, as a customer, are the centerpiece of it all. No arrangement that almost collects dust. No bored shopping assistant behind the desk. Every week is precious, every day, every hour because everyone knows this will not last forever. There is also the element of improvisation. What has been arranged in the morning might sell out and be replaced by something else. Items are arranged in a way that feels right intuitive. Born out of the gut feeling of the wonderful people running the show rather than a centrally mandated planogram. These pop-up stores intend to make money and sell; however, there is something more to it. They want you to leave the world changed. To orchestrate a shopping experience that lasts and has a long after-taste. They want to make every visit special.

THE GREAT RETURN

And that's precisely the same feeling that you can enjoy at some conferences. It seems that the online years have leveled the playing field of physical conferences with only two groups surviving and thriving: the big ones with thousands of participants, big names, and concert-like perfect execution, and the small ones that are being born out of the initiative and motivation of a small group of enthusiasts. The latter often does not use established event locations but transforms industrial and corporate locations into pop-up events. Tape art instead of fixed installations. Little surprises all along the way. A small card on the buffet table. A quote on the mirrors of the washrooms that you don't expect but makes you smile. All helping hands behave like the staff in a pop-up store, wanting you to feel comfortable. Understand and feel the event's purpose and bring inspiration and new ideas home. Feelings that a later download of the presentation decks or video recordings will not be able to capture and transmit. To make this a special day. A unique day. Something that most likely cannot be repeated. Magic of the moment while being together with others.

What if we were to transform a day in the office into a pop-up day? Into something special? What if we tried to steal the concept we have seen and experienced in temporary stores across Seoul, Toronto, Shanghai, L.A., Berlin, Tokyo, and many other places, trying to create the same magic we have experienced at great conferences outside the corporate halls? Wouldn't it be worth a try?

THE GREAT RETURN

Questions for reflection:

1. What is your fondest memory from a pop-up store that you ever set foot in?

2. What conference in the past two years resonated well with you and why?

3. What would be an excellent occasion to interrupt the regular flow in a corporate office environment?

4. What would it take for your team to feel like not being at the office while being at the office?

18 SHIFTING THE PERSPECTIVE

For over a year, there have been intense discussions on what employers can do. Can they order people back to the office after years of remote work? What are the rights of employees in this? Can they insist on working from home rather than returning to the office? As outlined before, entering such a debate is not the purpose of this book. However, one thought might be valuable for our endeavor to facilitate a move back to the office—a thought experiment.

What if we turn this around and, instead of asking if 'people have a right to remain in the home office' ask if 'people have a right to demand their colleagues to return to the office'?

Doesn't that make sense? Put yourself in the shoes of someone who joined the workforce recently. Straight out of university. Wouldn't that person have the right to an intense personal onboarding and enjoy all the gifts of working together in person? Being introduced to a colleague because this person just happened to walk by. Receiving a little hand-written note after a long day where everything seemed to have gone wrong. Experiencing the first performance review in life not through a screen but by being in the same room as your leader, seeing a group holding the space for one team member with a weak moment, and feeling the magic of genuine collegial support.

Or imagine somebody else wanting to bounce off an idea that is too fresh and undefined to justify scheduling a meeting but might hold great potential to turn into something significant, where a slight glance, a small early input, and a perspective might change the course of the whole thing. All it would take in the office would be a 'knock on the door' and 30 seconds.

THE GREAT RETURN

What if someone is being recognized for having taken the extra mile for the company and delivered far beyond what was expected? To provide standing ovations to this unsung hero. Yes, we can send flowers to the private address, and there are thousands of emoticons in virtual collaboration tools. Still, a room full of enthusiastic people applauding for 3 minutes will simply feel different and create memories that far outweigh the monetary award. There are so many more examples that highlight the motivation to request colleagues to return to the office.

Questions for reflection:

1. If you think about the people around you, has anyone ever asked colleagues to return to the office?

2. When and where would be an excellent opportunity to discuss this in the team you are a member of?

3. Please name three requests/reasons for each team member to come to the office without hesitation.

THE GREAT RETURN

19 TAKING IT SLOW

We all have different ways to react to changes in our environment. Some adapt faster; others take more time before feeling comfortable again. You might know individuals constantly preparing mentally for several 'what if' scenarios. In contrast, others dance through the day with a smile on their faces, embracing every change as the 'happy new normal' within the shortest time. Personality, education, profession, nature, and nurture all play a role. One aspect of diversity as well. Hence, some adapt faster to change, and others need more time.

It's interesting to observe Olympic athletes in training. Despite their superb physical condition, they would never enter a short workout session without taking time for a good warm-up. To get their bodies ready for what's to come. Because even if there would be no harm in 95 out of 100 cases, the 5 percent of cases that go wrong are not worth the risk.

Suppose we assume each team member must arrive back at the office well. In that case, we need to take time to adjust to the sudden increase in noise, to the different (artificial) lighting, to have no opportunity for a short nap that used to be a great energy booster before hitting an afternoon full of calls, to being in a room with many other people and feeling simply overwhelmed by all the energy and things going on at the same time. Remember the first time you walked into a crowded pachinko parlor in Japan? This is what spending a day at the office feels like for many.

Hence, it might be a good idea not to go full throttle on your first day. Start with a small dose and then increase. Give yourself a chance to adapt and develop tolerance again. Part (office) time.

THE GREAT RETURN

Questions for reflection:

1. What is an intelligent way to plan for breaks throughout the day?

2. What would it take to signal others that you have reached your limit?

20 BEING GRATEFUL

If you are holding this book in your hands, chances are high that you are privileged. Even to be allowed to think about where you spend your time working is a luxury to many colleagues who can only contribute when they are at a specific location at a particular point in time. They have no choice. To them, hybrid work is not on the table. Not even by far.

Our point here is not to discuss solidarity but to take a moment to rest and reflect on what responsibility comes along with this privilege to have a say in the design of hybrid work. Not to be forced to spend every day operating a machine, to fix things, to move things, to serve others in service functions limited to the physical person to person world. We acknowledge that what we face now is a 'luxury problem'. It might feel overwhelming, and our worries and fears are accurate; however, putting them in perspective is a good practice.

THE GREAT RETURN

Questions for reflection:

1. What would change if you only were allowed to work from within the corporate perimeter?

2. Imagine you would have to present your state of mind and plan about hybrid work choices to a group of machine operators, what would you say?

3. What obligations arise from this?

21 NO ONE GETS LEFT BEHIND

If you go through all the people you used to have conversations with before we left for the digital offices at home and compare them to your current contacts list, you might find several people missing. Some might have left the company, others took on new jobs in another division far away, and that's the natural flow of things. However, there might also be some people who have become more and more silent over the past few years. Who started to keep communication to a minimum and who probably lost the smiles on their faces. The ones we honestly can't say how they're doing if someone inquires. Single data points will show up in any associate surveys on employee engagement or not if they have drifted off so far as not to care anymore.

With more and more of us returning to the office, we can ensure they aren't left behind. The opportunity to invite them back to join the group. To feel a sense of belonging again. Not summoned through the sharp sound of a whistle but with gentleness. A soft-spoken invite. Encouragement. Support along the first steps. And we might be rewarded with a glow in their eyes and contributions that leave us in awe.

THE GREAT RETURN

Questions for reflection:

1. Who are the first three names on your list?

2. What would be the warmest welcome for each of them?

THE GREAT RETURN

22 LEADERS ON A HYBRID SHIP

There is no easy answer to the dominant leadership style we are facing right now. You will find role models on the spectrum between transactional and transformational approaches and a fluid demand from an ever more diverse workforce. Now, throw three places of work into the mix, and we will end up with a reasonably large solution space. Everyone has an opinion on how others should do it, and they are not shy of articulating on social media 24/7.

How about leaders ask themselves some fundamental questions:

1. What is my default mode of leading (natural state)?

2. How has my leadership style changed in the past 36 months?

3. How can I ensure everyone knows how I want to play delegation poker in the next 12 months?

THE GREAT RETURN

23 ACCIDENTS AT THE OFFICE

Things are going wrong in all three worlds. In the home office, corporate office, and places in between.

Someone might forget to unmute for the third time in a row, and everyone starts laughing, including that person. The first time a pet ran across a screen, it made our faces smile. Or the latest virtual collaboration software misunderstands gestures and starts to send pulsing hearts or thumbs up across the screen at the most inappropriate moment. These moments are valuable because they give us a free shot of endorphin, dopamine, and oxytocin. Happy teams, profit beams.

And now, imagine all the fun that awaits us at the corporate office. Two people miss a nano-second and simultaneously enter the automated revolving doors. They find themselves trapped in a small space, shuffling like penguins along with the door moving until they are rereleased into freedom. Or two people pressing the button of a coffee machine at the same time. The 10th person enters a meeting room that is double booked, says sorry, and then comes back 5 minutes later with a box of fresh doughnuts. We realized that a painting had been hanging upside down for the past five years, and we had never noticed—misunderstandings in conversations. People mix up languages and start choosing the wrong one, with people needing help understanding a word. It also results in laughter and sparking joy on a rainy day.

THE GREAT RETURN

Questions for reflection:

1. When was the last time you had a really good laugh at the corporate office?

2. What would it take to make this a regular one?

24 THE ILLUSION OF GLOBAL WORK

The moment we switched to virtual-only communication, the world seemed to become flat. A dream was coming true in leveling the playing field. Inclusion of colleagues in faraway locations in a way that was unprecedented before. No more meetings with most people sitting in the same room and some having to dial in to take a seat in the 2nd row. Now, everyone went online. Same chances to take part in discussions. No electronically raised hand passing the line when talking. Each comment on the electronic whiteboard has the same chance of being seen of being discussed. And it gave people who lacked advanced rhetoric skills a voice. Everyone could comment in the chat and through the power of 'thumbs up' and 'hearts', chances were high to vote things into the spotlight of discussion that did not have a chance of prominence before.

This would facilitate global team setup and allow us to make a dream come true: bringing global teams to life. No more restrictions in leveraging a workforce around the globe. Being able to staff and collaborate as we never have done before.

And then we realized that, while the virtual skills we acquired helped significantly, the dream did not fully come true. We underestimated that we still work across time zones and that even with all the best intentions, there are very few hours every day where everyone can tune in (from any location). Leaving us sitting at the early morning table or replacing a starlight virtual background with a real one. And we continued to face challenge number two: cultural differences. While we all now share the same fate of being forced into our homes for a while, we still bring along all aspects that make cultures collide.

THE GREAT RETURN

Nuances that get missed include very different views on 'good leadership practices', ways of communicating and forming an opinion, and finding consensus, even down to the question of who should join which circle at which point in time. And now, with us returning to office, this might even amplify because of local self-enforcement of rituals and norms that shift the focus and attention on what is right in front of your face. Most likely, it's not even a lousy intention, but it might be due to the excitement of being in the same room(s) again, thereby forgetting about our international friends. They fade away on the horizon. Step by step by step...

Questions for reflection:

1. How can we preserve a way to feel connected globally?

2. What is the right level of taking teams globally with all we know now? How would we design things differently if we were to do it again?

3. How can we leverage the uniqueness and beauty of regional differences?

THE GREAT RETURN

25 MICRO SABBATICALS

It seems that leaving things behind and taking a 'Gap Year' has gained broad acceptance since we left for the home office. Once a phenomenon of Western students' rite of passage and a sign of affluence, exposing ourselves to a very different environment for a limited period is regarded as a viable tool to recharge energy, gain different perspectives, and grow personally. We escape our daily schedules and make time to find back to ourselves. We check our priorities, reflect on what drives us, and get back in touch with ourselves. Or to immerse in a field of interest or obsession, like our academic friends have been practicing for centuries.

Unfortunately, there is no guarantee for sabbaticals to have a positive effect. We can easily spend 12 months away from the daily drumbeat and not feel significant change, while another 3-month break might be a genuinely transformative period for us. One of the critical success drivers is the ability to transition entirely into the 'other' world and suppress all that might disturb you. To cut all ties. To fully immerse.

And this brings us to a fascinating comparison with meditation. Using an excellent app, creating a perfect environment, and putting on your most comfy clothes will not guarantee you will clear your mind and find inner peace. It also hardly works when exercising with your mind for the first time. But after a while, you get better and need less time to reach the state of mind that you aspire to. You learn how to transition from one world into another, and even a couple of minutes every day might provide significant benefits and impact.

THE GREAT RETURN

So how can we use the three work modes (at home, at the office, and in-between) as 'micro-sabbaticals'? What would it take to choose locations so wisely that they feel like entering a different world that holds valuable treasures for us? What if all three locations had an inherent individual and distinct drumbeat that we could use as a refreshing impulse?

Questions for reflection:

1. What are good rituals to facilitate leaving one world behind and entering another one?

2. How can you reduce 'overspill' from one world into another?

3. What role can meditation practices play in this?

26 THE MOST WONDERFUL PARTY

If you think back about your teenage years. What guided you in deciding to accept an invitation to a party? Most likely, the feeling you had the last time you visited that friend's house was your guiding light. Did you feel happy the last time you went there? Does a smile cross your face when you think back? What feelings does the last party evoke?

So why would things be different a decade or two later? What if we, instead of forcing people back to work, would try to create irresistible invitations? What if we provoke undeniable great experiences that lead to people wanting to return to get more of them? What if things were to take place at the corporate office, which feels so great that we don't want to miss out on them again?

Questions for reflection:

1. What is the fondest memory you have from a day at the office?

2. What could be good advice for recreating such an event?

3. Who in your circle of influence would be a key enabler/partner in crime for this?

THE GREAT RETURN

27 RIDING TO SCHOOL TOGETHER

Depending on which part of the world you grew up in, your way to school might have looked very different. But let's assume that you somehow shared the daily commute with other kids. Be it on the school bus, your bike, a train, in the back of some parents' car, or by walking. These daily journeys might have taken you through some rural areas or made you experience considerable city traffic. They might have been short or felt like forever. Some are more exposed to changing seasons, some with constant weather conditions and the corresponding dress code.

Assuming the minimum age of the readers of this guide is 20, you will all still remember a time when we did not have to care about reception along the way and spoke to each other, when we discussed things of the highest importance, like an unexpected change in a series on TV, a party that will take place next week, a hint for the upcoming test. Or when you used the time together to get something off your chest. To get some feedback and perspective. Support. Or to be in the role to lend others your ear. Or to fall in love and make that time together in the morning the most important minutes of the day.

What if we were to make use of our commutes for that again? Not to hold on to the 'good old days' but to use the face-to-face time that is so precious—riding to work together, walking and talking while we find our way through enormous city labyrinths—turning the routine into something that we will remember 20 years from now. Like the stories of us riding to school together when we were young.

THE GREAT RETURN

Questions for reflection:

1. Who of your colleagues shares part of your morning journey?

2. What if you walked the last part of our commute?

3. Who of your neighbors is heading out in the same direction as you?

THE GREAT RETURN

28 MIRRORS ON THE WALL

Lets talk about feedback. Having moved to the zeitgeist of good leadership attributes, we love to hear from others about their perspective on us. We are not caring so much about the likes on social media but good, honest, rich feedback as a gift.

And the best way to harvest such feedback is in written form. It trumps oral input in several ways. First, we can stop reading and digest what has been written. Start to reflect. When someone is talking to you, hitting the mute button will, in the best cases, interrupt the flow and, in the worst case, eliminate a great source of feedback for you. Second, we can rewind and reread the feedback. Allowing for better understanding. Third, we can look back after a while and enjoy the great feeling of improving things. Or to check if we are still working on the right things. Or take out some great feedback we received and use it on a rainy day to make the clouds disappear. Fourth, some people are better at being honest when writing (primarily if things are written anonymously). We usually know who we speak to. Fifth, some characters like to structure their thoughts and take some time before providing feedback. It's easier to take notes than restructure to end up with a beautifully written format. Hence, there are five good reasons why written feedback has advantages.

However, the world is not black and white, and there might also be an argument for verbal feedback. For once, it's more effort to write things than to simply speak. Using the five minutes you walk from a joint meeting back to the desk or the 90 seconds in the elevator. And some individuals, despite all promises of anonymity, might be hesitant to put things in writing. Some feelings of not wanting to be quoted, and evidence exists that chances for verbal feedback are higher when you meet face to face. Just think about the last time you saw someone and said, 'Good to see you; what I wanted to tell you … '. Hence, bumping into somebody might be a feedback-provoking trigger.

Questions for reflection:

1. How has your feedback behavior changed in the past three years (giving and receiving)?

2. What is your preferred place to provide feedback (at home, at the office, in-between)?

3. What are valuable practices for giving/receiving feedback in a virtual space and person?

29 MAKEUP

It is a widespread assumption that there are two main reasons for putting makeup on. One motivator for spending nonsignificant parts of our disposable income on small substances of all shapes and sizes is covering up things we don't like. Either concealing them or emphasizing other things, i.e., distracting the viewer's eye. Probably not to get rid of things entirely but to 'massage the truth' to some extent. To make things less obvious. To blur. To apply a visual filter.

Another key argument for using makeup is to transform into something else. To put a mask on. To morph into our 'working visual self'. Probably supported by a morning ritual, we become what we want to be step by step. It's still us, but it's an intentional version that will appear on a virtual screen or in person.

Hence, makeup allows us to put a distance between the 'real us' and the view of the world on us—a protective barrier.

And now, we are wondering about people's backgrounds when joining virtual meetings. How much of that is covering something up that we don't want? How much of this reinforces an image that we want to portray?

THE GREAT RETURN

Questions for reflection:

1. How do your daily rituals differ from one working mode to another?

2. How has your appearance changed in the past 24 months?

3. What if somebody were to ban all make-up and background screens from earth?

30 IT IS NOT ABOUT YOU

Let us assume that you have figured it all out for yourself. You have found your perfect hybrid mix for the years to come. Either because the nature of your work determines a specific drumbeat. Or because you have a rock-solid conviction about which type of task you perform best in which environment. Or you belong to one of the three 'exclusive clubs' and only go for one working mode.

And we applaud you for that. You are very close to unleashing the most productive you going forward. The only challenge is that, most likely, people are joining you. Chances are high that you work together with others. Be it loosely or having your team members as part of your daily standup routines. Their hybrid dream should also be considered to ensure the whole orchestra delivers an outstanding performance. Hence, it will be about synchronizing and, most likely, compromise. Not to give up the excellent environments that each individual thrives in but to find a way to allow them to co-exist over time.

Some colleagues still need to understand their optimal hybrid mix clearly. Be it because they are new to the work world or are still reflecting and experimenting. They are a couple of steps behind you on their word-mode learning curve. Wouldn't it be great if they could learn from you? Hear your side of the remote work story. Stand on your shoulders that you have been through endless great and frustrating experiences. Not to make them fans of your hybrid cocktail but to provide perspective.

And probably, while sharing your personal best practice of designing your work days, you will start to question one or the other thing again…

THE GREAT RETURN

Questions for reflection:

1. Is everyone in your environment aware of your preferred hybrid blueprint and the reasons behind it?

2. Which parts of your future dream schedule are engraved in stone, and where do you still have question marks?

3. What is an excellent way to communicate your personal preferences?

31 BUSINESS TRAVEL 2.0

While in the early 2000s, frequent flyer luggage tags were genuine badges of honor, this picture has changed a lot. The two 'online only' years have left lasting marks on us, and we have realized that we can achieve a lot purely virtually.

When reviewing all the past trips, we would be more hesitant to jump on the next plane to meet with colleagues across the globe. Abundance has led to complacency in choosing when to meet in person and seek out virtual alternatives. We took the trip. Connecting virtually often has been regarded as a '2nd best', a 'backup solution'. It's probably also a sign of not valuing our conversation partners enough. Just a virtual meeting instead of the 'real thing'.

And now? How do we throw business travel into the hybrid mix? Going forward, we have one significant advantage: person-to-person interaction is more scarce and, thereby, more valuable. We have something to look forward to. We might also use every minute of being together to be with each other because time together is precious. People leave their laptops behind when traveling because they only talk to people and do not check their email while away—ending the day with a sundowner at the bar to start the day again with a morning walk and a personal conversation. 24/7, using the fact that we can sense and feel each other. There is no need to waste valuable meeting time to present or convey information. That can be done at ease and very efficiently in a virtual pre-meeting.

THE GREAT RETURN

Time travel to the days when we walked to the harbor in the morning to see if the expected ship arrived with our guests and, if not, to return the next day. And when it finally did, we enjoyed every moment and were lucky that we could see each other unharmed and that they had a safe journey.

Questions for reflection:

1. How can you redesign your and your guest's travel agendas to use every personal minute?

2. How do we steal from the concept of 'blended learning' to have part of the meeting virtually, then physically return to the virtual space for an after-session?

3. Name three trips from your past that make your eyes glow when talking about them. What made them so special?

32 A NEUTRAL PLACE

If you talk to interior designers about the most significant headache they face when creating corporate mavens, it's 'future readyness'. While it's safe to assume that corporations will soon be able to have sound estimates about the collective work schedules of their associates and will be able to plan for how many people will show up per location per day, the big two unknowns seem to be the development of individual preferences and changing roles.

With AI not scratching the surface of today's job descriptions, no one knows how work will change in the next decade. What part of today's work should we delegate? Where do we stay in the loop? Where do we want to control things? How much alignment and exchange will be needed? All of that will determine the physical office layout that supports each shade of white-collar laptop-induced knowledge work.

Another challenging animal is individual preference. Do we expect to find our little home office decor mimicked in the corporate office space? How would that look like, given hundreds of individual tastes? Should the design language of the corporate office scream 'neutral zone' and avoid any attempt to make things personal and comfortable? And how will this evolve? How much should a company provide, and how much should the associates have a say in the design of the office spaces? The corporate office as our canvas? How do we balance personal preference with the wish to bring the unifying corporate brand to life? How do you maintain a visual identity over time?

THE GREAT RETURN

Questions for reflection:

1. What are your expectations of a perfect office environment now?

2. What could be the guiding principles to make this future-proof?

3. What is a great industry to learn from?

33 A DAY IN THE CITY

Some folks might enjoy this guide while looking out the window onto lush greens and the countryside, enjoying the 'good life' away from noisy and combusted downtown streets where things are running at a different pace: less anonymity, less crazy rent, less crime, fewer crowds, and traffic jams. There are good reasons to keep a healthy distance from the pulsing hearts of our metropolitan dreams. One might even argue that the benefits of home office working modes have been far more significant when working from home in the countryside than their urban colleagues.

We hypothesize that this group of rural colleagues has a unique opportunity to turn a trip to an urban office location into something special, like our predecessors, who rode in a horse wagon to a pioneering city in the late 19th century. Some of these days are calls of duty, but there is more. An opportunity to explore things that are not part of the everyday life. A particular restaurant for lunch, an art exhibition opening in the evening, and a little pop-up store to stroll by. A different crowd. A different pulse. The opportunity to design a day that holds so much more than just spending hours in the corporate office halls. And when the sun goes down, leave all the hustle behind again and savor the return home. Transition back into a beautiful world of quiet. To then already looking forward towards the next time…

THE GREAT RETURN

Questions for reflection:

1. How can you make each day at the corporate office something special?

2. When did you last check for cultural events around your office location?

3. What is one small thing you can take from your trip to the office back home, like a slice of cake from that particular bakery?

THE GREAT RETURN

34 A LITTLE BIT OF NOTHING

Fusion is a beautiful concept, not only in food. It is combining things that have been separated before to create something new. To enrich experiences. To blend and recreate. Athleisure Wear. Workstations. Glamping. Brunch, Edutainment, Mocktails. All combine the 'best of two worlds' to deliver something one cannot do alone—a brilliant concept.

Until it is overdone. Feature-overkill. You are trying too hard and taking it one step too far. Do you remember being unable to order a regular cup of coffee at a coffee shop anymore? Do you need half an hour to find classic chanting songs for yoga practice on your streaming app without electronic beats that aim to create a beach clubby feeling? When it becomes too much? When blending things leaves you with less than before. Only some emulsions are good ideas.

And the same holds for working from home, working from the office, and places in between. Please try to resist the temptation to turn all three into a little bit of each other. Love and use them for their strengths rather than trying to stretch them to something they are not. Embrace them for what they are. Non-diluted excellence for certain types of work at a certain point in time. Protecting the great by not diluting, by refraining from throwing everything into the hybrid mixer.

THE GREAT RETURN

Questions for reflection:

1. What would be the perfect task for each of the three working modes?

2. Have you ever decided to say 'no' and exclude yourself instead of applying the wrong mode for the task?

3. How has your view changed in the past year?

THE GREAT RETURN

35 PRESENTS

Before Corona, we gathered often to celebrate. An anniversary, someone getting married, someone leaving the company, heading for the next adventure.

And there has been a typical protocol for such events. Step 1: everyone gathers in an open space or meeting room. Step 2: a series of announced speeches (with or without notes in hand). Step 3: a minimum of one speech that has yet to be announced beforehand and that typically leads to loud and hard laughter. Step 4: give full attention to the person of interest with a short speech, including a handover of drinks and food. Step 5: increase noise levels to the usual 70 dB while guests start talking to each other in small groups of 2-6. So far, so familiar. Steps 1-4, we have transferred somewhat to the online world, most prominently the live announcement. Step 5 (the gathering) we exercised during years of virtual year-end parties, but it never felt like 'the real thing'.

However, there has been one other thing we fell short of: presents. Spending weeks thinking and arguing about the most admirable and appropriate gift for the person of the day. How stories come up remembering the one or other thing that the person might have revealed about their preferences outside of work or articulated a need or a secret wish for a present. There are some things, after all, that shall only be gifted to you instead of you clicking a button yourself. We spend the same time selecting appropriate wrapping paper depending on the person. The whole room will then hold their breath and observe every micro-expression on the person's face to know if the present leads to the expected outcome.

THE GREAT RETURN

Questions for reflection:

1. How can we preserve beautiful gifting in virtual settings?

2. What is the next occasion that calls for some awesome gifting?

3. What are good ideas for presents that support an entire hybrid work lifestyle that jumps between locations?

36 BIG BANG THEORY

Fireworks have something in common. They always start with a big bang, like an antidote to a late 19th-century symphony that increases in volume, speed, and breadth over time to culminate in a grand finale. A firework is the other way around. Loud from the first minute on. Intense. High amplitude.

We believe that acknowledging the long absence from the office, people should be invited back with a big bang. A party to celebrate the re-opening of an abandoned office, a redesigned kitchen, an anniversary, a promotion, a newly established team, or a new hire. Bringing people together. In Person. Decoration. Music. Extraordinary. Over the top. Too much. A big bang to let us and others know that we are back.

Guided by the belief that such a big bang will make it easier to overcome doubt and hesitation. Something that carries you through the first steps back into the old (new) territory. To set a mark. Making each corner of the office more meaningful. To put a positive psychological anchor for each time you walk by the same place from now on.

Creating something that will be talked about. Not for a day, but for weeks and months. A bang that leaves a mark on the hearts and office furniture. Well-earned patina. A scratch on that surface is a witness to people using it—a stain on the carpet from a typical imbalance while dancing the evening away.

THE GREAT RETURN

Questions for reflection:

1. When was the last time you enjoyed a big bang in the office?

2. What would it take to recreate that moment?

3. What is the MVP (minimal viable party)?

THE GREAT RETURN

37 HAPPILY EVER AFTER

There is hardly a check-in at a hotel where you will not be informed about a special discount at the bar for a specific time of the day. The famous happy hour. A different crowd. Early evening. Before the dress code turns black and velvet. Casual. Two for one. A little more relaxed. The evening before Night. Special rules apply for 60 minutes. Special prices. Special drinks. Special atmosphere.

A regular meeting occasion at the bar across the street from the office? A short drink before taking the train home? One for the road? Mocktails. Nojito. Ginger Fizz. Virgin Mojito. Lightbulbs hanging over our heads. Everyone standing. Talking. Laughing. Well-balanced background music. And then we head out. To open another chapter for the evening. Workout. Dinner. A good book. Some grocery shopping. Transitioning into another world.

However, happy hours are not the only phenomenon that provokes reflection on hybrid work. How about 'after hours'? The party after the party? Extending an event by hanging out a little longer. A smaller crowd. Enjoying the mood of what took place before diminishing step by step. A unique atmosphere as well. Where servers grab a drink themselves, and the lines blur between guests and staff. Where things loosen up, stage heroes are becoming tangible. Imperfect. Showing a different side of themselves. There is no performance anymore. Everyone is leaving former roles behind. Actors, celebrities, listeners. It is time for deep conversations and asking all you did not dare before. Others just watch what unfolds in front of their eyes.

THE GREAT RETURN

No rules. Do what you like. No expectations. The 30 minutes after the show. The 30 minutes staying in the virtual meeting after some big announcement or intense discussions. After hours.

Questions for reflection:

1. Do you already make use of happy hours?

2. What would it take to establish a happy hour a) in the virtual space or b) in real life?

3. How do we cultivate 'secret' after hours that are not enforced but evolve naturally?

THE GREAT RETURN

38 SO MUCH WISER

Since we left the corporate office behind, we have learned so much. How can we avoid staying in meetings we did not belong to because we chose the wrong seat? Walking straight to the room and heading for the door would attract so much attention. Now, we could leave with a short note in the chat and one mouse click. And we did. Bravery. We take full ownership and responsibility for our time.

There are no excuses for procrastinating and binging an afternoon away at home just to feel so bad having put in half the night to make up for it and to meet that deadline: no one to blame but ourselves. No supervision. No one glancing at us or over our shoulders. The result of our work has never been more directly linked to our performance. No excuses.

We learned how to improvise and communicate despite unforeseen interruptions and little accidents. Sudden sunshine blinded us, requiring immediate relocation. Things that fell to the floor. Dozens of spilled bottles of water and coffee mugs.

And we learned how to stay calm and self-confident—activating the camera in the wrong moments. Machines in our homes make noises. Doorbells ring. Other people enter the scene unannounced and loudly. We learned how to 'own' all that—accepting our imperfections.

A significant teaching on how to stay in contact. Making an effort to reach out because relationships would have slipped away otherwise. And to pay attention. How do you interpret the smallest gesture? How do you look at the faces sitting on the other side of the virtual screen?

THE GREAT RETURN

We became so flexible and fast in taking new tools and features for a live test drive—no probation period. No training. No instruction. A new icon popped up out of nowhere every week. No problem. Lets give it a try.

In the home office, there has been no external protection from working too much. More than before, we had to become the guardians of our private life. An unprecedented level of discipline was required to maintain a healthy work-life balance. An ability to draw a boundary. Something many have been struggling with in the years before.

And there are many more examples. We are so much better than before. So much wiser. So much more capable.

THE GREAT RETURN

Questions for reflection:

1. What personal superpowers have you acquired in past two years (voluntary or because you had to)?

2. How can you leverage those going forward?

3. What is the best way to pass them on to your colleagues, team, mentees?

39 THE BIGGEST EXPERIMENT

Since VUCA accelerated in the past few years, definite answers are demanding. And even if there is some clarity on right or wrong, it won't stand up for long. It will only survive the first contact with a change that slaps us in the face.

Dialogue over the announcement. Harvesting the collective wisdom on an ongoing basis, hoping that one person in the room has the right idea at the right moment and that this voice is being heard. Tools and attitude help with that. Psychological safety is necessary, and appropriate meeting formats and communication increase the chances of success. So far, there is so much common sense, and it fits well with the current 'Leadership Zeitgeist'.

But we won't know for sure at the end of the day. We will have to stay flexible. We must be willing to adjust our plans to modify the hybrid mix. To shift between three locations. Accept that the times of stability might not return. That things will continue to flow.

If we accept all of the above, then we face an experiment. It is the most giant experiment of our working life. And if it's an experiment, then there is no reason not to embrace it fully with our best. With all we have to offer. It won't get better than this.

THE GREAT RETURN

Questions for reflection:

1. What is the worst thing that can happen if you make a mistake when designing your hybrid mix?

2. What guiding principles will always hold throughout the next 36 months?

THE GREAT RETURN

40 PERKS

These are not times to show off and discuss perks you enjoy. Understatement is the mantra of the 2020s. Bodyguards that blend into the crowd. Beneficiaries of Silicon Valley's Gilded Age ride five-figure Italian bicycles instead of jumping into a company limousine—the end of abundant corporate festivities with goodie bags full of premium swag to take home. No more corner offices and executive dining sections are a thing of the past during lunchtime. Less hierarchy. Shoulder to shoulder. Eye to eye.

Let's take stock of hybrid work for a minute. It somehow feels like 'perks for the masses'. Many corporations are investing heavily to bring you back to the office. New furniture and interior design, remodeled campuses, upgraded bike facilities, transportation subsidies, free yoga classes, mental health days, upgraded canteen menus, new Italian coffee bars, welcome back packages with branded luxury water bottles, chargers, guest lectures, relaxed office rules that allow bringing your pet along and the feeling that everyone is putting in extra effort to make you feel welcome back.

Aside from the things being thrown at you, how about free premium parking because you show up on a day and time that only a few others do? A super clean fridge and microwave for your homemade lunch, more bandwidth, and shorter lines at the IT service desk. And management might be more accessible, including more networking opportunities.

THE GREAT RETURN

Hence, there are tons of perks in your hands that have been beyond reach before.

Questions for reflection:

1. What three things make work at the corporate office more pleasant than before?

2. How can I make the best use of them?

THE GREAT RETURN

41 SUPERHEROES

Good leadership is fascinating. It comes along in various shapes and sizes. Some people enter the room and bring with them a calm confidence that makes you sail through every storm under their command. Others can eliminate every ounce of hierarchy and instill a feeling of absolute psychological safety and comfort. And then there are sparkling motivators. Their words quickly enter your head and heart, lifting you and making you feel stronger every minute listening to them. People who do not speak at all are on the other side of the spectrum. They are the masterminds behind strategies, and their logical thinking is breathtaking. Wake eyes. Brilliant minds.

Such leaders' power does not stem from their titles but the admiration they inspire in us. We are fascinated by their excellence. Respect truly earned, not given. Most of them manage to have this effect on many people, not a few and reconfirm this perception repeatedly. Just personality? Hardly. In most cases, decades of experience and training lead to a high level of unconscious competence.

And now it seems that there is a new breed in town. The hybrid superstars. Leaders who do not only manage to work their magic in person but in the virtual room as well. Those who keep up their shade of leadership excellence despite all challenges and shortcomings of working location and - mode. The deck is being reshuffled.

THE GREAT RETURN

Questions for reflection:

1. Who are your two superheroes of hybrid work?

2. How do they do it?

3. What are practices that you can steal from them with pride?

THE GREAT RETURN

42 THOSE KIND OF DAYS

There are those special days. Before washing machines, getting the laundry done involved significant preparation, and you would have to endure long hours of hard manual work. However, still today the task to 'get the laundry done' is perceived as laborious and, especially if you are pooling the fabrics of many people that scream for a good refreshing scrub, is often pre-planned and coordinated. Monday is laundry day. Friday is cleaning day. Saturday is market day.

And the world is better due to aligned schedules—more efficiency for once. Doing full loads of washing requires less energy and detergent. A weekly shopping trip to a particular neighborhood saves time and gas. However, such dedicated days create efficiency on the supply side as well. That special bread the bakery around the corner offers on Saturdays as an exclusive because the intense preparation is only justified with a certain amount of people craving it. Farmers coming to the city for a weekly market can access helping hands for setup and selling that they don't typically have on their payroll.

Another benefit of such coordination is peace of mind. We do not have to worry and to remember, like processes that waste CPU time, running in the back. All other days are 'no laundry days' and you can focus entirely on other things.

Traditions that are linked to one place. Being passed on to the next generation. Do as our organizational predecessors did or establish new ones that feel right and useful.

THE GREAT RETURN

Questions for reflection:

1. Are 'home office days', 'corporate office days', and 'outside days' already in place?

2. Are private 'days' in place that aim to align with professional 'days'?

3. Are the people around you aware of your regular schedule? Who else might benefit from knowing about it?

43 COLLECTIVE PLEDGES

Having formed an opinion on how you would stir up your hybrid work soup is only half the job. Unless you work in isolation, this thing will only fly if you find a way to coordinate with your corporate significant others. To enter a joint rhythm.

First, you have to make your thinking explicit. It's not an easy one, but it's worth it. Then, you have to find a way to exchange individual wishes. To discuss. To reflect. To adjust. And then, you should come to a point where your tribe/group/team comes to a set of agreements. A pledge that each team member signs. Such pledge should contain information about:

1. A minimal set of rules that are mandatory for everyone on the team.

2. A mechanism how to discuss and amend the pledge in case someone wishes to change.

3. How do we hold each other accountable? What happens if someone does not adhere to the rules?

THE GREAT RETURN

Questions for reflection:

1. What are the implicit rules of the team that exist already?

2. When did the team face a difficult situation to handle? What helped you back then, and how can you use it here?

3. How much of the rules are due to the nature of your work, and how much is due to the team's personalities?

44 WORKSHOP 365

Some years ago, when attending a corporate workshop, something interesting occurred. During the first coffee break, participants filled their pockets with food, drinks, pencils and grabbed stacks of notebooks. Not one at a time but in a hurry and with both hands full. That sparked my interest since none of the items were either of unique value or identified as fancy swag.

I observed the obscure incident for a while and then decided to put my Sherlock Holmes hat on and follow one of the bounty hunters. Where would he take the trophies of his raid? He went up the stairway to the first floor, entering an open office area. He walked straight up to the middle of the room, opened a cabinet, and started putting all the items very orderly. One by one. He was sorting them into what seemed to be the department's stationary vault. Then he saw me. Our eyes met, and he asked (assuming that I also worked for the company): 'Oh, sorry, do you need some of the stuff as well?'. What followed was a lovely conversation in which I learned about this special day. Whenever guests came for a workshop, the company was generous in passing out stationary, while on the other days of the year, it kept a very tight ship. Hence, different rules were applied when a workshop was being held.

Aside from tangible differences (free meals, swag), there is something else at work during work: a different atmosphere, a different setting. Something special in the way people talk to each other. An openness that is often lacking in the day-to-day. Room to contemplate. The feeling of people speaking from the heart, active and deep listening. People arrive with a different mindset and frame of thought for the day(s) the event takes place. After the event, everything goes back to normal again. How can we preserve what is so unique and precious about these dedicated events? How can we ensure we enjoy a workshop-like atmosphere 365 days per year?

Is it because the event is being announced ahead of time? Or that everyone is wearing name tags? The presence of moderators that are only sometimes around in the daily corporate life? The fact that tons of people are enjoying a coffee while standing around at precisely the same time? That the day have an explicit agenda/table of contents? That we learned, like Pavlov's dogs, that workshop time is a good time for focused work and exchange? That people pay full attention to their cell phones being tucked away in their pockets? If it's any of the above or the combination of many items, it seems that chances are good to recreate such an atmosphere regularly. What an intriguing idea.

THE GREAT RETURN

Questions for reflection:

1. How can you initiate/design/contribute to workshops and establish a new office traditions?

2. What are the hottest candidates for themes?

3. What makes your organization a prime candidate for this?

45 A FINAL WORD

Unfortunately, we will never know if our current way forward will be correct. If the current hybrid mix survives in the next 12 months, we must get together again to change and adjust. We hope that you have more clarity for yourself now. That you have a better idea of what will get the best out of you and the ones you work with. That it's not all black and white but about adding different flavors to our hybrid cocktails.

We hope these pages will make the transition easier for you and show that you are not alone and that many others feel like you do. The many that are struggling, questioning, and having mixed feelings about how the 'new hybrid' will look like, and that's ok.

And we hope this book has provided some confidence, nurtured the 'high spirits', and given you something to look forward to. Towards magical moments that we will remember for years to come. The one conversation that we carry in our hearts for months. That we also sparked some curiosity about how to reinvent ourselves in this hybrid environment and to find beauty in things.

An adventure is waiting for you… and us.

THE FIRST 30 DAYS DIARY

Day 1. Date:

What worked well?

What was difficult?

What to change?

Day 2. Date:

What worked well?

What was difficult?

What to change?

Day 3. Date:

What worked well?

What was difficult?

What to change?

Day 4. Date:

What worked well?

What was difficult?

What to change?

Day 5. Date:

What worked well?

What was difficult?

What to change?

Day 6. Date:

What worked well?

What was difficult?

What to change?

Day 7. Date:

What worked well?

What was difficult?

What to change?

Day 8. Date:

What worked well?

What was difficult?

What to change?

Day 9. Date:

What worked well?

What was difficult?

What to change?

Day 10. Date:

What worked well?

What was difficult?

What to change?

Day 11. Date:

What worked well?

What was difficult?

What to change?

Day 12. Date:

What worked well?

What was difficult?

What to change?

Day 13. Date:

What worked well?

What was difficult?

What to change?

Day 14. Date:

What worked well?

What was difficult?

What to change?

Day 15. Date:

What worked well?

What was difficult?

What to change?

Day 16. Date:

What worked well?

What was difficult?

What to change?

Day 17. Date:

What worked well?

What was difficult?

What to change?

Day 18. Date:

What worked well?

What was difficult?

What to change?

Day 19. Date:

What worked well?

What was difficult?

What to change?

Day 20. Date:

What worked well?

What was difficult?

What to change?

Day 21. Date:

What worked well?

What was difficult?

What to change?

THE GREAT RETURN

Day 22. Date:

What worked well?

What was difficult?

What to change?

Day 23. Date:

What worked well?

What was difficult?

What to change?

Day 24. Date:

What worked well?

What was difficult?

What to change?

Day 25. Date:

What worked well?

What was difficult?

What to change?

Day 26. Date:

What worked well?

What was difficult?

What to change?

Day 27. Date:

What worked well?

What was difficult?

What to change?

Day 28. Date:

What worked well?

What was difficult?

What to change?

Day 29. Date:

What worked well?

What was difficult?

What to change?

Day 30. Date:

What worked well?

What was difficult?

What to change?

ABOUT THE AUTHORS

We are passionate about the way people work. Being optimists at heart, we believe that the future holds great things. That we will master the return to the corporate halls and be able to orchestrate hybrid work in a way that leaves big smiles on our faces. We bring over 50 years of working experience to the table and still come out of a place of not knowing and being curious.

This book has been written by a person, not AI.

www.ingramcontent.com/pod-product-compliance
Lightning Source LLC
Chambersburg PA
CBHW071058240526
45471CB00016B/2155